This j

MW00931342

Hope is the thing with feathers
That perches in the soul,
And sings the tune without the words,
And never stops at all

Emily Dickinson

Disclaimer
This book is not intended to be a substitute for medical advice or treatment. Any person with a condition requiring medical attention should consult a qualified medical practitioner or suitable therapist.
The information provided in this book is stated to be truthful and consistent, in that any liability, in terms of inattention or otherwise, by any usage or abuse of any policies, processes, or directions contained within is the solitary and utter responsibility of the recipient reader. Under no circumstances will any legal responsibility or blame be held against the publisher for any reparation, damages, or monetary loss due to the information herein, either directly or indirectly.

The 365
Addiction Recovery Journal

Declaration Of Intent

This journal is created with our utmost care and the honest intention to give lasting benefit to you, the owner of this book. The power of journaling, of consistent self-reflection, is a scientifically proven habit that will benefit your life in truly astonishing ways. Nothing is so detrimental to addiction as genuine self-inquiry. Therefore we've created a top-quality guided journal to help you on your journey of self-discovery. Because if you stop wasting potential, mainly talents, integrity, and love, your world soon will be a better place.

As a little thank you note,
we've three **Free** Personal-Growth exercises waiting for you.

Simply send an email to to exercises21@yahoo.com
Title the email "Recovery"

And we will send you Three Personal Development Hacks for Free.

Because of the success of this journal, we've collaborated with self-help author C.W. V. Straaten, and added the first chapter of his
The Addiction Recovery Workbook: A 7-Step Master Plan To Take Back Control Of Your Life to this journal.

You can find this chapter at the end, after Day 365.

The 365 Addiction Recovery Journal

Daily Journaling With Guided Questions,
To Become A New You.

---

21 EXERCISES

Follow us on Instagram

For promotions, giveaways and newest arrivals

Instagram:
21exercises_journals

Introduction

Your Journey Begins

Addiction is not the end. If it's anything, it is the beginning of a new era. There is darkness. A big hole of dirt, of pain. You've seen the end. You've faced destruction, faced evil. And still, you're here. It hasn't pulled you down. You're alive. You're still standing. Braver, stronger, taller, and more beautiful than ever. Isn't being in recovery an absolute superpower? Facing the dark and still standing in the light. Think about what you can accomplish with this superpower. The possibilities are endless.

Wherever you are on your recovery path, don't forget about that. You are developing a superpower. You aren't a former addict, but a developing superhuman. Make your lessons count, take one step at a time, and bring joy, color, and laughter back into your life. By buying this book, you've decided to take a massive step forward. Daily journaling is a magical habit. The continuous reflection will bring you growth and happiness. We want to thank you for making that step, and we're cheering for you on your journey wherever it may go.

Don't let the music die in you.

How To Use This Journal

Instructions For The Journey.

1. It's time to start your 365 Journey. Turn the page.
2. Don't be intimidated by any *how-to's*. Use your own wisdom. The writing prompts are not designed to use it one specific way. Just give it your best shot.
3. Try to be honest. If there is one thing that can dissolve addictive behavior, it is honesty. Awareness. That's the first step to change.
4. No phone, no distractions. Help yourself by putting genuine attention in using the writing prompts. Just set aside 5 to 15 minutes a day for your journaling exercise. You can do a short meditation before doing your journaling exercise. Give yourself the attention you deserve, and for 5 to 15 minutes a day create a moment that's totally for *you.*
5. Remember, you can't make mistakes here. If you are looking for a direction, it's this: write down your first impulse and be brutally honest. It is your own private journal of self-discovery.
6. And be kind to yourself. You've taken a beautiful step by buying this journal and with your intention of doing daily journaling. That alone is worth a celebration.
7. Okay, that's it. Good luck and above all, enjoy:)!

"The unthankful heart discovers no mercies; but the thankful heart will find, in every hour, some heavenly blessings."
Henry Ward Beecher

Day 1 - Describe the moment you realized you were addicted.

_____

_____

_____

_____

_____

_____

_____

_____

_____

_____

_____

Day 2 - Write a response to your younger self for this thought: "But I can't do without...(for example drinking game/smoking weed/gambling)."

_____

_____

_____

_____

_____

_____

_____

_____

_____

_____

"Rock bottom became the solid foundation on which I rebuilt my life."
J.K. Rowling

Day 3 - List the three most inspiring things that caused you to question your addictive behavior.

_____

_____

_____

_____

_____

_____

_____

_____

_____

_____

_____

Day 4 - How could you help yourself to express yourself more authentically?

_____

_____

_____

_____

_____

_____

_____

_____

_____

"To live is so startling it leaves little time for anything else."
Emily Dickinson

Day 5 - Write a response to your addiction for this thought:
"Why put so much energy in recovery?"

_____
_____
_____
_____
_____
_____
_____
_____
_____
_____
_____

Day 6 - Write down all the critical thoughts you have about
yourself. Let them out. Release them.

_____
_____
_____
_____
_____
_____
_____
_____
_____

"I am not afraid of storms, for I am learning how to sail my ship."
Louisa May Alcott

Day 7 -List five things that don't matter so much if you were going to die within two months.

_____

_____

_____

_____

_____

_____

_____

_____

_____

_____

Day 8 - Do you have a recovery plan?

_____

_____

_____

_____

_____

_____

_____

_____

_____

_____

"The reward of a thing well done is having done it."
Ralph Waldo Emerson

Day 9 - Describe a typical pattern that led/leads to your addictive behavior.

_____

_____

_____

_____

_____

_____

_____

_____

_____

_____

_____

_____

Day 10- Come up with three simple solutions to break this pattern before you relapse.

_____

_____

_____

_____

_____

_____

_____

_____

_____

"Fear of joy is the darkest of captivities."
Phil Kaye

Day 11 - What have you tried to escape with your addiction?

_____

_____

_____

_____

_____

_____

_____

_____

_____

_____

Day 12 - What would you ask your 80-year-old self?

_____

_____

_____

_____

_____

_____

_____

_____

_____

_____

"Then you must teach my daughter this same lesson. How to lose your innocence but not your hope. How to laugh forever."
Amy Tan

Day 13 - What would he or she answer?

_____

_____

_____

_____

_____

_____

_____

_____

_____

_____

Day 14 - If your addiction was a person, what would his or her characteristics be?

_____

_____

_____

_____

_____

_____

_____

_____

_____

"Look. I have a strategy. Why expect anything? If you don't expect anything, you don't get disappointed."
Patricia McCormick

Day 15 - Look at yesterday's answer, what could you learn from this addiction person'?

_____

_____

_____

_____

_____

_____

_____

_____

_____

_____

_____

Day 16 - If being in recovery were a superpower, what else could you do with this superpower?

_____

_____

_____

_____

_____

_____

_____

_____

_____

"It's the possibility that keeps me going, not the guarantee."
Nicholas Sparks

Day 17 - Write a response to your younger self for this thought:
"I am destined for misery."

_____

_____

_____

_____

_____

_____

_____

_____

_____

_____

Day 18 - If you had to choose one affirmation to live by this
week, what would it be?

_____

_____

_____

_____

_____

_____

_____

_____

_____

"If at first the idea is not absurd, then there is no hope for it."
Albert Einstein

Day 19 - What are the five things you hate the most about your addiction?

_____

_____

_____

_____

_____

_____

_____

_____

_____

_____

_____

Day 20 - What are your weak spots where it's easy for addiction to enter?

_____

_____

_____

_____

_____

_____

_____

_____

_____

"Hope in reality is the worst of all evils because it prolongs the torments of man."
Friedrich Nietzsche

Day 21 - What would be an excellent habit to have to help you live a calmer life?

_____

_____

_____

_____

_____

_____

_____

_____

_____

_____

_____

Day 22 - Look at yesterday's answer. How could you integrate this habit in your life, starting today?

_____

_____

_____

_____

_____

_____

_____

_____

_____

"To pay attention, this is our endless and proper work."
Mary Oliver

Day 23 - Write down three lessons from your addiction years.

_____
_____
_____
_____
_____
_____
_____
_____
_____
_____

Day 24 - Describe your ideal week.

_____
_____
_____
_____
_____
_____
_____
_____
_____
_____

"Perhaps the rare and simple pleasure of being seen for what one is compensates for the misery of being it."
Margaret Drabble

Day 25 - List 5 people you're incredibly grateful for.

_____
_____
_____
_____
_____
_____
_____
_____
_____
_____
_____

Day 26 - What would you regret not saying if you were going to die today?

_____
_____
_____
_____
_____
_____
_____
_____
_____

"Do you not see how necessary a world of pains and troubles is to school an intelligence and make it a soul?"
John Keats

Day 27 - List three things you're too tough on yourself during recovery.

_____

_____

_____

_____

_____

_____

_____

_____

_____

_____

_____

Day 28 - What people in your life have a mostly negative impact on you?

_____

_____

_____

_____

_____

_____

_____

_____

"We learn from failure, not from success!"
Bram Stoker

Day 29 - What does a day without addiction look like?

_____

_____

_____

_____

_____

_____

_____

_____

_____

Day 30 - Commit to treating yourself this week. Write down what and how you're going to do it.

_____

_____

_____

_____

_____

_____

_____

_____

_____

_____

"Truths are written, never said... Lines are drawn, but then they fade."
Colleen Hoover

Day 31 - Make a timeline of your addiction with the memories you find important

_____

_____

_____

_____

_____

_____

_____

_____

_____

_____

_____

Day 32 - Write down all the negative thoughts you have about love. Let them out. Release them.

_____

_____

_____

_____

_____

_____

_____

_____

"The more I read, the more I acquire, the more certain I am that I know nothing."
Voltaire

Day 33 - Look at yesterday's answer and write down the positive counterparts for a maximum of five negative statements. Do it in a way that works for you. For example, 'Nobody will ever really love me," to "I give love and open to receive love."

_____

_____

_____

_____

_____

_____

_____

_____

_____

_____

_____

Day 34 - Give three statements to encourage yourself when life gets tough.

_____

_____

_____

_____

_____

_____

"'Never, never, never give in!"

Day 35 - How could spirituality help you during your recovery?

_____

_____

_____

_____

_____

_____

_____

_____

_____

_____

_____

Day 36 - If your addiction was a person, what would he or she look like?

_____

_____

_____

_____

_____

_____

_____

_____

_____

_____

_____

The older I grow, the more I distrust the familiar doctrine that age brings wisdom.

Day 37 - Describe one memory you're incredibly grateful for. This question will return later in this journal, to integrate an attitude of gratefulness.

_____

_____

_____

_____

_____

_____

_____

_____

_____

Day 38 - Describe your addictions in 7 words.

_____

_____

_____

_____

_____

_____

_____

_____

_____

_____

_____

"We live in an age when unnecessary things are our only necessities."

Oscar Wilde

Day 39 - Take the seven words from yesterday and write down the positive counterparts applicable to you — for example, impatience - confidence.

_____
_____
_____
_____
_____
_____
_____
_____
_____
_____
_____
_____

Day 40 - Write about your past ambitions.

_____
_____
_____
_____
_____
_____
_____
_____
_____
_____
_____

"I think I've discovered the secret of life — you just hang around until you get used to it."

Day 41 - Write down three affirmations to empower your recovery.

_____

_____

_____

_____

_____

_____

_____

_____

_____

Day 42 - Three things you would like to say yes to.

_____

_____

_____

_____

_____

_____

_____

_____

_____

"Authority without wisdom is like a heavy axe without an edge, fitter to bruise than polish."
Anne Bradstreet

Day 43 - How has addiction affected your love life?

_____
_____
_____
_____
_____
_____
_____
_____
_____

Day 44 - What would be the one thing you wish could be fulfilled today?

_____
_____
_____
_____
_____
_____
_____
_____
_____
_____
_____
_____

"Wonder is the beginning of wisdom."
Socrates

Day 45 - List three people you're (a tiny bit) jealous of and why.

_____

_____

_____

_____

_____

_____

_____

_____

_____

_____

Day 46 - How did your family shape you positively? Write down at least three things.

_____

_____

_____

_____

_____

_____

_____

_____

_____

_____

_____

"Sometimes one likes foolish people for their folly, better than wise people for their wisdom."
Elizabeth Gaskell

Day 47 - How did your family shape you negatively? Write down at least three things.

_____

_____

_____

_____

_____

_____

_____

_____

_____

Day 48 - Write a response to your critical self for this thought: "Don't be so weak."

_____

_____

_____

_____

_____

_____

_____

_____

_____

_____

"Common sense in an uncommon degree is what the world calls wisdom."
Samuel Taylor Coleridge

Day 49 - In what ways did your addiction shape you positively?

_____

_____

_____

_____

_____

_____

_____

_____

_____

Day 50 - What small thing would make your life so much easier?

_____

_____

_____

_____

_____

_____

_____

_____

_____

_____

_____

"Life would be tragic if it weren't funny."
Stephen Hawking

Day 51 - What is missing in your life?

_____
_____
_____
_____
_____
_____
_____
_____
_____

Day 52 - What is abundant in your life?

_____
_____
_____
_____
_____
_____
_____
_____
_____
_____
_____
_____

"Half of seeming clever is keeping your mouth shut at the right times."
Patrick Rothfuss

Day 53 - Describe the opposition of addiction.

Day 54 - Why is integrity important?

"My imagination makes me human and makes me a fool; it gives me all the world and exiles me from it."
Ursula K. Le Guin

Day 55 - What would an ideal start of your day (first one hour) look like?

_____

_____

_____

_____

_____

_____

_____

_____

_____

Day 56 - Look at yesterday's answer. Try to incorporate this morning routine for seven days. Write down one thing you are going to do right now to make sure you will follow through (ie: setting the alarm).

_____

_____

_____

_____

_____

_____

_____

_____

_____

"Risks must be taken because the greatest hazard in life is to risk nothing."
Leo F. Buscaglia

Day 57 - At the end of the week, review your morning ritual. What were your main takeaways? Even if you didn't follow through, write down your main takeaways and why you didn't follow through.

_____

_____

_____

_____

_____

_____

_____

Day 58 - What is your self-image?

"Never complain, never explain. Resist the temptation to defend yourself or make excuses."
Brian Tracy

Day 59 - What are the benefits of giving?

_____

_____

_____

_____

_____

_____

_____

_____

_____

Day 60 - What are the benefits of receiving?

_____

_____

_____

_____

_____

_____

_____

_____

_____

_____

_____

"Be faithful in small things because it is in them that your strength lies."

Day 61 - If you were the master of your own addiction, what would you tell it?

_____

_____

_____

_____

_____

_____

_____

_____

_____

_____

Day 62 - How has addiction affected your relationship with your family?

_____

_____

_____

_____

_____

_____

_____

_____

_____

_____

"One resolution I have made, and try always to keep, is this: 'To rise above little things'."
John Burroughs

Day 63 - What are the benefits of letting go of desire?

_____

_____

_____

_____

_____

_____

_____

_____

Day 64 - What are the benefits of letting go of resistance?

_____

_____

_____

_____

_____

_____

_____

_____

_____

_____

_____

_____

"At what point do you give up – decide enough is enough? There is only one answer really. Never."

Tabitha Suzuma

Day 65 - A thought experiment: give one simple solution to stay in recovery.

_____

_____

_____

_____

_____

_____

_____

_____

_____

_____

Day 66 - What frequently overwhelms you?

_____

_____

_____

_____

_____

_____

_____

_____

_____

"The Revolution introduced me to art, and in turn, art introduced me to the Revolution!"
Albert Einstein

Day 67 - What do you like about nature?

_____
_____
_____
_____
_____
_____
_____
_____
_____
_____

Day 68 - How has addiction affected your relationship with your friends?

_____
_____
_____
_____
_____
_____
_____
_____
_____
_____

"Anything under God's control is never out of control."
Charles Swindoll

Day 69 - What are your top three priorities in life?

_____

_____

_____

_____

_____

_____

_____

_____

_____

_____

_____

Day 70 - What one easy thing could you do to improve your
health this week?

_____

_____

_____

_____

_____

_____

_____

_____

_____

_____

_____

"Where there is no hope, it is incumbent on us to invent it."
Albert Camus

Day 71 - Describe your favorite way to express yourself.

_____
_____
_____
_____
_____
_____
_____
_____
_____
_____
_____

Day 72 - What is your favorite strategy to deal with (escaping) uncomfortable situations?

_____
_____
_____
_____
_____
_____
_____
_____
_____
_____

"Hopes are like hair ornaments. Girls want to wear too many of them. When they become old women they look silly wearing even one."
Arthur Golden

Day 73 - What do you like to do for relaxation?

_____

_____

_____

_____

_____

_____

_____

_____

_____

_____

Day 74 - Give the one question you'd desperately want to ask your addiction.

_____

_____

_____

_____

_____

_____

_____

_____

_____

_____

"All of a sudden, this shooting star went by, and all I could think was that they were listening to us somehow. "
Nicholas Sparks

Day 75 - How would it answer?

Day 76 - What would you love to achieve shortly?

"The only way of knowing a person is to love them without hope."
Walter Benjamin

Day 77 - What careers are you most curious about?

_____
_____
_____
_____
_____
_____
_____
_____
_____
_____
_____

Day 78 - Can you forgive yourself for your addiction? Why or why not?

_____
_____
_____
_____
_____
_____
_____
_____
_____
_____
_____

"Man suffers only because he takes seriously what the gods made for fun."
Alan Wilson Watts

Day 79 - If your life was a movie, what kind of movie character would you be? Describe your movie character?

_____
_____
_____
_____
_____
_____
_____
_____
_____
_____
_____
_____

Day 80 - What three things do you wish you knew ten years ago?

_____
_____
_____
_____
_____
_____
_____
_____
_____
_____
_____

"All the darkness in the world
cannot extinguish the light of a single candle."
St. Francis Of Assisi

Day 81 - What hidden talents might you have?

_____

_____

_____

_____

_____

_____

_____

_____

_____

Day 82 - If you had to follow your instinct, what one major
decision would you make?

_____

_____

_____

_____

_____

_____

_____

_____

_____

You have made quite a journey already.

Take a moment to recognize it.

To breathe in and embrace your progress.

"One is not born, but rather becomes, a woman."
Simone de Beauvoir

Day 83 - Sit down for five minutes. Set the alarm. In silence, reflect on your thoughts. Review afterward: what are your thoughts? Words, sounds, sensations? And where do they come from?

_____
_____
_____
_____
_____
_____
_____
_____
_____
_____

Day 84 - If your thoughts were different, what would you do?

_____
_____
_____
_____
_____
_____
_____
_____
_____

"I would never die for my beliefs because I might be wrong."
Bertrand Russell

Day 85 - List three things that make you feel uncomfortable.

_____

_____

_____

_____

_____

_____

_____

_____

_____

Day 86 - What is a better way to handle your painful emotions?

_____

_____

_____

_____

_____

_____

_____

_____

_____

_____

_____

_____

_____

"A wounded deer leaps the highest"
Emily Dickinson

Day 87 - Write down at least three reasons why your addictive behavior is irrational.

_____

_____

_____

_____

_____

_____

_____

_____

_____

_____

_____

Day 88 - How do you respond to making a mistake?

_____

_____

_____

_____

_____

_____

_____

_____

_____

_____

_____

"Perhaps home is not a place but simply an irrevocable condition."
James Baldwin

Day 89 - What would you regret not hearing if you were going to die today?

Day 90 - Write down three things you feel grateful for in your life.

"The most incomprehensible thing about the world is that it is at all comprehensible."
Albert Einstein

Day 91 - How do you deal with boredom?

_____

_____

_____

_____

_____

_____

_____

_____

_____

_____

Day 92 - Describe the ideal version of yourself when it comes to finances.

_____

_____

_____

_____

_____

_____

_____

_____

_____

_____

"One of the penalties of refusing to participate in politics is that you end up being governed by your inferiors."
Plato

Day 93 - Look at yesterday's answer. Write down at least one experience where your actions resembled the best version of yourself when it came to finances. What can you learn from this experience?

_____

_____

_____

_____

_____

_____

_____

_____

Day 94 - What are three of your best character traits?

_____

_____

_____

_____

_____

_____

_____

_____

_____

_____

_____

_____

"I'm restless. Things are calling me away. My hair is being pulled by the stars again."
Anaïs Nin

Day 95 - What does fear mean to you?

_____
_____
_____
_____
_____
_____
_____
_____
_____

Day 96 - What does strength mean to you?

_____
_____
_____
_____
_____
_____
_____
_____
_____
_____
_____

"Things do not change; we change."
Henry David Thoreau

Day 97 - What one easy thing could you do to improve your mental wellbeing this week?

_____

_____

_____

_____

_____

_____

_____

_____

Day 98 - What are you grateful for right now?

_____

_____

_____

_____

_____

_____

_____

_____

_____

_____

_____

"Wisest is she who knows she does not know."
Jostein Gaarder

Day 99 - How can you make someone's day today?

_____
_____
_____
_____
_____
_____
_____
_____
_____
_____

Day 100 - Where would you be right now, if you didn't commit to recovery?

_____
_____
_____
_____
_____
_____
_____
_____
_____
_____
_____

The journey is what brings us happiness not the destination."
Dan Millman

Day 101 - What are the benefits of cleaning up your house regularly?

_____

_____

_____

_____

_____

_____

_____

_____

_____

_____

Day 102 - What does someone need to believe to continue addictive behavior?

_____

_____

_____

_____

_____

_____

_____

_____

_____

_____

The flame that burns Twice as bright burns half as long."
Lao Tzu

Day 103 - How would you describe mindfulness?

_____
_____
_____
_____
_____
_____
_____
_____
_____
_____

Day 104 - Write a response to your younger self for this thought: "Recovery is so boring, you've got to enjoy life."

_____
_____
_____
_____
_____
_____
_____
_____
_____
_____

"I don't deserve a soul, yet I still have one. I know because it hurts."
Douglas Coupland

Day 105 - What can you do to strengthen your recovery today?

_____

_____

_____

_____

_____

_____

_____

_____

_____

Day 106 - What would you like to say about yourself one year
from now?

_____

_____

_____

_____

_____

_____

_____

_____

_____

"What you are is God's gift to you, what you become is your gift to God."
Hans Urs von Balthasar

Day 107 - What would you like to have accomplished one year from now?

_____
_____
_____
_____
_____
_____
_____
_____
_____

Day 108 - What is the biggest enemy of recovery? How can you deal with it?

_____
_____
_____
_____
_____
_____
_____
_____
_____

"I know many lives worth living."
Mary Oliver

Day 109 - Write a response to your younger self for this thought:
"I will never be able to recover from... (example:
drinking/overeating/playing video games)."

Day 110 - Write down all the negative thoughts you have about
this world. Let them out. Release them.

"Some people talk in their sleep. Lecturers talk while other people sleep"
Albert Camus

Day 111 - Describe your inner child.

_____
_____
_____
_____
_____
_____
_____
_____
_____
_____

Day 112 - Describe your critical self.

_____
_____
_____
_____
_____
_____
_____
_____
_____
_____
_____

"As long as the sun's shining, shit can't be that bad."
J. Lynn

Day 113 - When was the last time you've laughed about yourself?

_____

_____

_____

_____

_____

_____

_____

_____

_____

_____

_____

_____

Day 114 - What could other people in recovery learn from you?

_____

_____

_____

_____

_____

_____

_____

_____

_____

"Hope itself is like a star– not to be seen in the sunshine of prosperity, and only to be discovered in the night of adversity. "
C.H. Spurgeon

Day 115 - How would you treat a loved one who is addicted?

_____

_____

_____

_____

_____

_____

_____

_____

_____

_____

_____

Day 116 - How would you treat a loved one who is in recovery?

_____

_____

_____

_____

_____

_____

_____

_____

_____

_____

_____

"But hoping," he said, "is how the impossible can be possible after all."
Marissa Meyer

Day 117 - Do you fear to lose your identity by being in recovery?

_____

_____

_____

_____

_____

_____

_____

_____

_____

_____

Day 118 - How can you gain more power over your addictive behavior?

_____

_____

_____

_____

_____

_____

_____

_____

_____

_____

"With every mistake, we must surely be learning."
George Harrison

Day 119 - What pleasant surprise did you discover today?

_____
_____
_____
_____
_____
_____
_____
_____
_____
_____
_____

Day 120 - A thought experiment: give a straightforward solution that would've saved you from the horrors of addiction.

_____
_____
_____
_____
_____
_____
_____
_____
_____

"Keep a little fire burning; however small, however hidden."
Cormac McCarthy

Day 121 - Describe a moment when you overcame failure.

_____
_____
_____
_____
_____
_____
_____
_____
_____
_____
_____
_____

Day 122 - Write down a more positive explanation for 'failure'.

_____
_____
_____
_____
_____
_____
_____
_____
_____
_____

"That night when you kissed me, I left a poem in your mouth, and you can hear some of the lines every time you breathe out."
Andrea Gibson

Day 123 - Write down all your negative thoughts about success.

_____

_____

_____

_____

_____

_____

_____

_____

_____

_____

Day 124 - Look at yesterday's answer and write down the positive counterparts for a maximum of five negative statements. Do it in a way that works for you. For example, "Success is not for me," to "I am a success magnet."

_____

_____

_____

_____

_____

_____

_____

_____

_____

_____

"We promise according to our hopes and perform according to our fears."
François de La Rochefoucauld

Day 125 - How would you like to be remembered?

_____
_____
_____
_____
_____
_____
_____
_____
_____
_____
_____
_____

Day 126 - Write a response to your younger self for this thought:
"I am so afraid of what other people think of me."

_____
_____
_____
_____
_____
_____
_____
_____
_____

"What I want is so simple I almost can't say it: elementary kindness."
Barbara Kingsolver

Day 127 - How can tomorrow be a better day?

_____

_____

_____

_____

_____

_____

_____

_____

_____

_____

Day 128 - How can you practice feeling better without relying on external forces?

_____

_____

_____

_____

_____

_____

_____

_____

_____

_____

_____

"To wish was to hope, and to hope was to expect"
Jane Austen

Day 129 - When was the last time you said, "I can't,"? Why?

_____
_____
_____
_____
_____
_____
_____
_____
_____
_____
_____
_____

Day 130 - What pleasant surprise did you discover this week?

_____
_____
_____
_____
_____
_____
_____
_____
_____
_____

"Honesty is the first chapter of the book wisdom."
Thomas Jefferson

Day 131 - What made you feel proud today?

Day 132 - Write a response to your addiction for this thought: "But you don't understand how I feel."

"It is one thing to be clever and another to be wise."
George R.R. Martin

Day 133 - What do you most frequently need to feel better?

_____
_____
_____
_____
_____
_____
_____
_____
_____
_____

Day 134 - What one easy thing could you do to improve all areas
of your life this week?

_____
_____
_____
_____
_____
_____
_____
_____
_____
_____

*"If we encounter a man of rare intellect,
we should ask him what books he reads."*
Ralph Waldo Emerson

Day 135 - Do you often feel better than others? Why or why not?

_____

_____

_____

_____

_____

_____

_____

_____

_____

_____

_____

Day 136 - What motivates you to recover from addiction?

_____

_____

_____

_____

_____

_____

_____

_____

_____

_____

"Time is a game played beautifully by children."
Heraclitus

Day 137 - Describe your own feeling of stress.

_____
_____
_____
_____
_____
_____
_____
_____
_____
_____

Day 138 - When was the last time you complimented yourself?

_____
_____
_____
_____
_____
_____
_____
_____
_____
_____
_____

"Having children makes you no more a parent than having a piano makes you a pianist."
Michael Levine

Day 139 - Write down how you could help yourself after a relapse without being self-critical.

_____

_____

_____

_____

_____

_____

_____

_____

_____

_____

Day 140 - How did your viewpoints about addiction change in the past few years?

_____

_____

_____

_____

_____

_____

_____

_____

_____

_____

_____

"A wise man will make more opportunities than he finds."
Francis Bacon

Day 141 - When was the last time you've laughed so hard it hurt?

_____
_____
_____
_____
_____
_____
_____
_____
_____
_____
_____

Day 142 - What three lessons did you learn last week?

_____
_____
_____
_____
_____
_____
_____
_____
_____
_____
_____

Remember, it's never too late who you might have been.

"And the most beautiful words ever spoken, I have not yet said to you."
Nazım Hikmet

Day 143 - How do you feel about a to-do-list?

_____

_____

_____

_____

_____

_____

_____

_____

_____

_____

_____

Day 140 - What apologies do you still want to make?

_____

_____

_____

_____

_____

_____

_____

_____

_____

_____

_____

_____

"The public have an insatiable curiosity to know everything,
except what is worth knowing."
Oscar Wilde

Day 145 - What memory are you very embarrassed about?

_____
_____
_____
_____
_____
_____
_____
_____
_____
_____
_____
_____
_____

Day 146 - What would you love to tell the people closest to you?

_____
_____
_____
_____
_____
_____
_____
_____
_____
_____
_____

"You shall create beauty not to excite the senses
but to give sustenance to the soul. "
Gabriela Mistral

Day 147 - What would you love to tell the rest of the world?

_____

_____

_____

_____

_____

_____

_____

_____

_____

_____

_____

Day 148 - Describe one memory you're incredibly grateful for.

_____

_____

_____

_____

_____

_____

_____

_____

_____

_____

_____

"The soul becomes dyed with the colour of its thoughts."
Marcus Aurelius

Day 149 - What pleasant surprise did you discover this year?

_____

_____

_____

_____

_____

_____

_____

_____

_____

_____

_____

Day 150 - Are your short-term actions and long-term goals still aligned?

_____

_____

_____

_____

_____

_____

_____

_____

_____

_____

_____

"The essence of being human is that one does not seek perfection."
George Orwell

Day 151 - What one easy thing could you do to improve your self-esteem this week?

_____
_____
_____
_____
_____
_____
_____
_____
_____
_____

Day 152 - Write a response to your addiction for this thought:" This recovery thing is just out of

_____
_____
_____
_____
_____
_____
_____
_____
_____
_____

*"The only man who never makes mistakes
is the man who never does anything."*
Theodore Roosevelt

Day 153 -When was the last time you complimented someone else?

_____

_____

_____

_____

_____

_____

_____

_____

_____

Day 154 - How did your viewpoints about spirituality change in the past few years?

_____

_____

_____

_____

_____

_____

_____

_____

_____

"Every strike brings me closer to the next home run."
Babe Ruth

Day 155 - Write a response to your younger self for this thought: "My life will never change."

_____

_____

_____

_____

_____

_____

_____

_____

_____

_____

Day 156 - How would an ideal end of your day (last one hour) look like?

_____

_____

_____

_____

_____

_____

_____

_____

_____

_____

"Happiness consists in frequent repetition of pleasure"
Arthur Schopenhauer

Day 157 - Look at yesterday's answer. Try to incorporate this evening routine for seven days. Write down one thing you are going to do right now to make sure you will follow through (ie: setting the alarm).

_____

_____

_____

_____

_____

_____

_____

_____

_____

Day 158 - After a week, review your evening routine. What were your main takeaways? Even if you didn't follow through, write down your main takeaways and why you didn't follow through.

_____

_____

_____

_____

_____

_____

_____

_____

_____

_____

"The eye sees only what the mind is prepared to comprehend."
Robertson Davies

Day 159 - Write down all the negative thoughts you have about the people in your life.

_____

_____

_____

_____

_____

_____

_____

_____

_____

_____

_____

Day 160 - Write a response to your critical self for this thought: After receiving a compliment, "They don't really mean it."

_____

_____

_____

_____

_____

_____

_____

_____

_____

"It is strange how a scrap of poetry works in the mind and makes the legs move in time to it along the road." "
Virginia Woolf

Day 161 - Describe one memory you're incredibly grateful for.

_____

_____

_____

_____

_____

_____

_____

_____

_____

_____

Day 162 - Write a response to your younger self for this thought: "I feel horrible now, and I don't see any way out."

_____

_____

_____

_____

_____

_____

_____

_____

_____

_____

*"The cosmos is within us. We are made of star-stuff.
We are a way for the universe to know itself."*
Carl Sagan

Day 163 - Write down all the negative thoughts about health.

_____

_____

_____

_____

_____

_____

_____

_____

_____

_____

Day 164 - Look at yesterday's answer and write down the
positive counterparts for a maximum of five negative statements.
Do it in a way that works for you. For example, "Living the green
lifestyle is just not for me," to "My body is my temple, and I take
good care of it."

_____

_____

_____

_____

_____

_____

_____

_____

_____

_____

"I don't want to be a tree; I want to be its meaning."
Orhan Pamuk

Day 165 - What did you learn today?

_____
_____
_____
_____
_____
_____
_____
_____
_____
_____
_____
_____

Day 166 - How can you hold yourself accountable while being in recovery?

_____
_____
_____
_____
_____
_____
_____
_____
_____
_____

"The first method for estimating the intelligence of a ruler is to look at the men he has around him."
Niccolò Machiavelli

Day 167 - What are the benefits of being patient?

_____
_____
_____
_____
_____
_____
_____
_____
_____
_____
_____
_____

Day 168 - How can you practice patience?

_____
_____
_____
_____
_____
_____
_____
_____
_____
_____

"Don't explain your philosophy. Embody it."
Epictetus

Day 169 - How can you practice forgiving yourself more easily?

_____
_____
_____
_____
_____
_____
_____
_____
_____
_____
_____

Day 170 - Write a response to your addiction for this thought:
"Why can't I just enjoy life."

_____
_____
_____
_____
_____
_____
_____
_____
_____
_____

"On the whole human beings want to be good, but not too good,
and not quite all the time."
George Orwell

Day 171 - What have you always wanted to do but be ashamed to do it?

_____

_____

_____

_____

_____

_____

_____

_____

_____

Day 172 - Write a response to your younger self for this thought: "My dreams will never come true."

_____

_____

_____

_____

_____

_____

_____

_____

_____

_____

"You are an aperture through which the universe is looking at and exploring itself."
Alan Watts

Day 173 - What is something you've created in the past?

_____
_____
_____
_____
_____
_____
_____
_____
_____

Day 174 - Write a response to your critical self for this thought: After a date / first drinks with a stranger, "He/she is never going to call me again."

_____
_____
_____
_____
_____
_____
_____
_____
_____
_____

"The aim of art is to represent not the outward appearance of things, but their inward significance."
Aristotle

Day 175 - Do you find it hard to concentrate for more than 30 minutes? Why or why not?

_____

_____

_____

_____

_____

_____

_____

_____

_____

_____

Day 176 - What place always makes you feel calm?

_____

_____

_____

_____

_____

_____

_____

_____

_____

_____

_____

*"Whatever course you decide upon,
there is always someone to tell you that you are wrong."*
Ralph Waldo Emerson

Day 177 - Describe the ideal version of yourself when it comes to your physical appearance.

_____

_____

_____

_____

_____

_____

_____

_____

Day 178 - Look at yesterday's answer. Write down at least one experience where you felt physically attractive. What can you learn from this experience?

_____

_____

_____

_____

_____

_____

_____

_____

_____

_____

*"Laughter is not at all a bad beginning for a friendship,
and it is by far the best ending for one."*
Oscar Wilde

Day 179 - Write a response to your critical self for this thought:
"I am so socially awkward, no wonder people don't like me."

_____

_____

_____

_____

_____

_____

_____

_____

_____

_____

Day 180 - What questions can you ask yourself when you feel
overwhelmed?

_____

_____

_____

_____

_____

_____

_____

_____

_____

_____

"I don't know why we are here,
but I'm pretty sure that it is not in order to enjoy ourselves."
Ludwig Wittgenstein

Day 181 - Write a response to your addiction for this thought:
"You only live once."

_____

_____

_____

_____

_____

_____

_____

_____

_____

Day 182 - What can you do to strengthen your health this
month?

_____

_____

_____

_____

_____

_____

_____

_____

_____

_____

"All knowledge is worth having."
Jacqueline Carey

Day 183 -What questions can you ask yourself when you feel angry?

_____
_____
_____
_____
_____
_____
_____
_____
_____
_____
_____

Day 184 - Your favorite way to spend your day during addictive behavior.

_____
_____
_____
_____
_____
_____
_____
_____
_____
_____
_____

*"Wisdom is not a product of schooling
but of the lifelong attempt to acquire it."*
Albert Einstein

Day 185 - Five things that make you smile.

_____
_____
_____
_____
_____
_____
_____
_____
_____
_____

Day 186 - A moment in your life you'll never forget.

_____
_____
_____
_____
_____
_____
_____
_____
_____
_____

"He that breaks a thing to find out what it is has left the path of wisdom."
J.R.R. Tolkien

Day 187 - When you are in pain, what is the kindest thing you can do for yourself?

_____

_____

_____

_____

_____

_____

_____

_____

_____

Day 188 - How did your body try to tell you that it was time to quit your addiction?

_____

_____

_____

_____

_____

_____

_____

_____

_____

_____

"People who know little are usually great talkers,

while men who know much say little."
Jean Jacques Rousseau

Day 189 - What are the benefits of being humorous and lighthearted?

_____
_____
_____
_____
_____
_____
_____
_____
_____

Day 190 - What do you love about life?

_____
_____
_____
_____
_____
_____
_____
_____
_____
_____

"Love shall be our token; love be yours and love be mine. "

Day 191 - Three things you can do to increase your energy.

_____

_____

_____

_____

_____

_____

_____

_____

_____

Day 192 - Write down all the negative thoughts you have about money.

_____

_____

_____

_____

_____

_____

_____

_____

_____

_____

_____

_____

""He who is to be a good ruler must have first been ruled"

Day 193 - Look at yesterday's answer and write down the positive counterparts for a maximum of five negative statements. Do it in a way that works for you. For example, "Money is the root of all evil," to "The lack of money is the root of all evil."

_____

_____

_____

_____

_____

_____

_____

_____

_____

Day 194 - Three things you can do to increase your kindness towards others.

_____

_____

_____

_____

_____

_____

_____

_____

_____

_____

"It's not what you say out of your mouth that determines your life,

it's what you whisper to yourself that has the most power!"
Robert T. Kiyosaki

Day 195 - Write a response to your addiction for this thought:
"Just one last time."

_____

_____

_____

_____

_____

_____

_____

_____

_____

_____

Day 196 - Three things you would like to say no to.

_____

_____

_____

_____

_____

_____

_____

_____

_____

_____

_____

_____

"It takes a very long time to become young."

Day 197 - How can you be more self-responsible?

_____
_____
_____
_____
_____
_____
_____
_____
_____
_____

Day 198 - Seven words to describe your recovery.

_____
_____
_____
_____
_____
_____
_____
_____
_____
_____
_____

"Tread softly! All the earth is holy ground."

Christina Rossetti

Day 199 - Write a response to your younger self for this thought: "What direction should I follow?"

_____

_____

_____

_____

_____

_____

_____

_____

_____

Day 200 - Describe one memory you're incredibly grateful for.

_____

_____

_____

_____

_____

_____

_____

_____

_____

_____

_____

"I AM IGNORANT of absolute truth. But I am humble before my ignorance and therein lies my honor and my reward."
Khalil Gibran

Day 201 - Write a response to your younger self for this thought: "But I just can't do it."

_____
_____
_____
_____
_____
_____
_____
_____
_____

Day 202 - Two pieces of advice you would give to someone new in recovery.

_____
_____
_____
_____
_____
_____
_____
_____
_____
_____
_____

"Recognizing power in another does not diminish your own."
Joss Whedon

Day 203 - What are the benefits of being kind?

_____
_____
_____
_____
_____
_____
_____
_____
_____
_____
_____
_____

Day 204 - If you had to choose one affirmation to live by today or tomorrow, what would it be?

_____
_____
_____
_____
_____
_____
_____
_____
_____
_____
_____
_____

"A wise man gets more use from his enemies
than a fool from his friends."
Baltasar Gracian

Day 205 - What are the benefits of being optimistic?

_____
_____
_____
_____
_____
_____
_____
_____
_____
_____

Day 206 - How did your viewpoint about yourself change in the
past few years?

_____
_____
_____
_____
_____
_____
_____
_____
_____
_____
_____
_____
_____

"Hide not your talents, they for use were made,
What's a sundial in the shade?"
Benjamin Franklin

Day 207 - How did your friends shape you positively? Write down at least three things.

_____
_____
_____
_____
_____
_____
_____
_____
_____

Day 208 - When was the last time you said, "Nothing matters"? Why?

_____
_____
_____
_____
_____
_____
_____
_____
_____
_____
_____
_____

"The art of being wise is knowing what to overlook."
William James

Day 209 - How can you be more optimistic?

Day 210 - Write a response to your younger self for this thought:
"Please, help me."

"I'm kissing you now — across
The gap of a thousand years."
Marina Tsvetaeva

Day 211 - How did your addiction start?

_____
_____
_____
_____
_____
_____
_____
_____
_____
_____

Day 212 - Describe craving.

_____
_____
_____
_____
_____
_____
_____
_____
_____
_____
_____

"A smart person knows how to talk.
A wise person knows when to be silent."
Roy T. Bennett

Day 213 - Who is often controlling you?

_____
_____
_____
_____
_____
_____
_____
_____
_____
_____

Day 214 - What (kind of) charity would you like to support and why?

_____
_____
_____
_____
_____
_____
_____
_____
_____
_____

"The stupid neither forgive nor forget; the naive forgive and forget; the wise forgive but do not forget."
Thomas Szasz

Day 215 - What would you tell other people who suffer from addiction now?

_____

_____

_____

_____

_____

_____

_____

_____

_____

Day 216 - Describe your comfort zone.

_____

_____

_____

_____

_____

_____

_____

_____

_____

_____

_____

"A man is not called wise because he talks and talks again; but if he is peaceful, loving and fearless then he is in truth called wise."
Dhammapada

Day 217 - The three main differences between addiction and recovery.

_____

_____

_____

_____

_____

_____

_____

_____

_____

_____

Day 218 - What makes you feel embarrassed about addiction?

_____

_____

_____

_____

_____

_____

_____

_____

_____

_____

_____

Day 219 - Who or what makes you feel angry?

Day 220 - Describe the ideal version of yourself when it comes to love life.

"They all tell you not to fight fire with fire,
but that is only because they are afraid of your flames."
Caitlyn Siehl

Day 221 - Look at yesterday's answer. Write down at least one experience where your love or dating life was perfect. What can you learn from this experience?

_____
_____
_____
_____
_____
_____
_____
_____
_____

Day 222 - What would you regret not seeing if you were going to die today?

_____
_____
_____
_____
_____
_____
_____
_____
_____
_____

"Come friends, it's not too late to seek a newer world."
Alfred Lord Tennyson

Day 223 - Describe something you once liked that you now dislike.

_____

_____

_____

_____

_____

_____

_____

_____

_____

_____

Day 224 - Describe something you once disliked that you now like.

_____

_____

_____

_____

_____

_____

_____

_____

_____

"Happiness is part of who we are. Joy is the feeling"
Tony DeLiso

Day 225 - Make a timeline of your recovery with the memories
you find essential.

_____

_____

_____

_____

_____

_____

_____

_____

_____

Day 226 - How did your viewpoints about friendships changed
in the past few years?

_____

_____

_____

_____

_____

_____

_____

_____

_____

_____

_____

"Death is the easy part, the hard part is living and knowing you could be so much more than you're willing to be."
Robert M Drake

Day 227 - Write down three things you could easily do to be a better friend to yourself.

_____

_____

_____

_____

_____

_____

_____

_____

Day 228 - Do one thing this week to step out of your comfort zone. It can be as simple as trying out a different route back from work. Write down what you're going to do and when.

_____

_____

_____

_____

_____

_____

_____

_____

_____

"Everything that is done in this world is done by hope."
Martin Luther

Day 229 - Describe the ideal version of yourself when it comes to expressing yourself.

_____

_____

_____

_____

_____

_____

_____

_____

_____

Day 230 - Look at yesterday's answer. Write down at least one experience where you felt expressing yourself made you feel important. What can you learn from this experience?

_____

_____

_____

_____

_____

_____

_____

_____

_____

_____

"Sadness is but a wall between two gardens."
Kahlil Gibran

Day 231 - What made you feel grateful today?

_____
_____
_____
_____
_____
_____
_____
_____
_____
_____

Day 232 - When was the last time you said, "I don't care"? Why?

_____
_____
_____
_____
_____
_____
_____
_____
_____
_____
_____

"You'll stop hurting when you stop hoping."
Guillaume Musso

Day 233 - Why do you deserve better in life?

_____
_____
_____
_____
_____
_____
_____
_____
_____

Day 234 - Did you do something out of your comfort zone this week? If so, how did it make you feel? What can you learn from it? If you didn't, write down a short plan for how you're going to do it this week.

_____
_____
_____
_____
_____
_____
_____
_____
_____

"We live in an age when unnecessary things are our only necessities."
Oscar Wilde

Day 235 - What are you willing to do to live a more calm and peaceful life?

_____

_____

_____

_____

_____

_____

_____

_____

_____

Day 236 - Write about your courage.

_____

_____

_____

_____

_____

_____

_____

_____

_____

_____

_____

"Farewell Hope, and with Hope farewell Fear"
John Milton

Day 237 - Write down a confession of one of your deep down secrets that you can't tell anyone.

_____

_____

_____

_____

_____

_____

_____

_____

_____

Day 238 - How would you like to improve your home/room?

_____

_____

_____

_____

_____

_____

_____

_____

_____

_____

"I would rather be a man of paradoxes than a man of prejudices."
Jean-Jacques Rousseau

Day 239 - What are you willing to do to achieve your most important goal(s)?

_____
_____
_____
_____
_____
_____
_____
_____
_____
_____

Day 240 - Seven words to describe your weakest self.

_____
_____
_____
_____
_____
_____
_____
_____
_____
_____
_____
_____
_____

"Even in the mud and scum of things, something always, always sings."
Ralph Waldo Emerson

Day 241 - What would you like to learn about addiction?

_____
_____
_____
_____
_____
_____
_____
_____
_____
_____

Day 242 - What would you like to learn about recovery?

_____
_____
_____
_____
_____
_____
_____
_____
_____
_____
_____

"Man is always prey to his truths.
Once he has admitted them, he cannot free himself from them."
Albert Camus

Day 243 - Describe the ideal version of yourself when it comes to your social life (family).

_____

_____

_____

_____

_____

_____

_____

_____

_____

Day 244 - Look at yesterday's answer. Write down at least one experience where your social life (family) was perfect. What can you learn from this experience?

_____

_____

_____

_____

_____

_____

_____

_____

_____

"The best revenge is not to be like your enemy."
Marcus Aurelius

Day 245 - Write a response to your addiction for this thought: "It wasn't so bad."

_____

_____

_____

_____

_____

_____

_____

_____

Day 246 - What makes addiction ridiculous?

_____

_____

_____

_____

_____

_____

_____

_____

_____

_____

_____

_____

"If you place your head in a lion's mouth, then you cannot complain one day if he happens to bite it off."
Agatha Christie

Day 247 - What would you like to learn about success?

_____

_____

_____

_____

_____

_____

_____

_____

_____

_____

Day 248 - Write a response to your addiction for this thought: "If nobody finds out, it's okay."

_____

_____

_____

_____

_____

_____

_____

_____

_____

_____

"Take it easy, but take it."
Woody Guthrie

Day 249 - What questions can you ask yourself when you feel fear?

_____
_____
_____
_____
_____
_____
_____
_____
_____

Day 250 - Who do you admire and why?

_____
_____
_____
_____
_____
_____
_____
_____
_____
_____

No single event can awaken within us a stranger whose existence we had never suspected. To live is to be slowly born."
Antoine de Saint-Exupéry

Day 251 - What would you like to learn about finances?

_____
_____
_____
_____
_____
_____
_____
_____
_____
_____
_____

Day 252 - Write down all the negative thoughts about your physical appearance.

_____
_____
_____
_____
_____
_____
_____
_____
_____
_____

"The highest activity a human being can attain is learning for understanding, because to understand is to be free."
Baruch Spinoza

Day 253 - Look at yesterday's answer and write down the positive counterparts for a maximum of five negative statements. Do it in a way that works for you. For example, "I am too short," to "I feel comfortable and sexy in my own skin."

_____

_____

_____

_____

_____

_____

_____

_____

_____

Day 254 - How can you use money instead of time to solve your most pressing problem?

_____

_____

_____

_____

_____

_____

_____

_____

_____

_____

"Stop feeling sorry for yourself and you will be happy."
Stephen Fry

Day 255 - What can you do to strengthen your recovery this
week?

_____

_____

_____

_____

_____

_____

_____

_____

_____

_____

Day 256 - How is social media affecting your self-esteem?

_____

_____

_____

_____

_____

_____

_____

_____

_____

_____

_____

"Fair speech may hide a foul heart."
J.R.R. Tolkien

Day 257 - What did you learn about yourself today?

_____

_____

_____

_____

_____

_____

_____

_____

_____

_____

Day 258 - Write a response to your critical self for this thought: "This (negative) always happens to me."

_____

_____

_____

_____

_____

_____

_____

_____

_____

_____

_____

"The end may justify the means as long as there is something that justifies the end."
Leon Trotsky

Day 259 - What is the one small thing you want to do today that would make you feel proud?

_____

_____

_____

_____

_____

_____

_____

_____

_____

Day 260 - What is one thing you would do differently when you look at last week?

_____

_____

_____

_____

_____

_____

_____

_____

_____

_____

_____

_____

"A great many people think they are thinking when they are merely rearranging their prejudices."
William James

Day 261 - Write a response to your addiction for this thought: "I easily can stop anytime I want."

_____

_____

_____

_____

_____

_____

_____

_____

_____

_____

Day 262 - What would you regret not feeling if you were going to die today?

_____

_____

_____

_____

_____

_____

_____

_____

_____

"Into the darkness they go, the wise and the lovely. "
Edna St. Vincent Millay

Day 263 - Describe one memory you're incredibly grateful for.

_____
_____
_____
_____
_____
_____
_____
_____
_____
_____

Day 264 - Will recovery ever become easier? Why or why not?

_____
_____
_____
_____
_____
_____
_____
_____
_____
_____
_____

"Wisdom comes to us when it can no longer do any good."
Gabriel García Márquez

Day 265 - Do you find it hard to tell other people that you're in recovery? Why or why not?

_____

_____

_____

_____

_____

_____

_____

_____

_____

_____

Day 266 - Write a response to your critical self for this thought: After achieving a big result, "I could have done better."

_____

_____

_____

_____

_____

_____

_____

_____

_____

_____

"All good things are wild and free."
Henry David Thoreau

Day 267 - What are you ashamed of about yourself?

_____

_____

_____

_____

_____

_____

_____

_____

_____

_____

Day 268- What could you improve from today?

_____

_____

_____

_____

_____

_____

_____

_____

_____

_____

"Love is the poetry of the senses!"
Honoré de Balzac

Day 269- Write down five things that trigger your addictive behavior.

_____
_____
_____
_____
_____
_____
_____
_____
_____

Day 270- Did you learn about new triggers this week? If so, what are they?

_____
_____
_____
_____
_____
_____
_____
_____
_____
_____
_____
_____

*"Nothing contributes so much to tranquilize the mind
as a steady purpose"*
Mary Shelley

Day 271 - What would you like to learn about love?

_____

_____

_____

_____

_____

_____

_____

_____

_____

_____

Day 272 - Do you still feel guilty about your addictive behavior?
Why or why not?

_____

_____

_____

_____

_____

_____

_____

_____

_____

_____

"Through endless night the earth whirls toward a creation unknown..."
Henry Miller

Day 273 - What does relapse mean to you?

_____
_____
_____
_____
_____
_____
_____
_____
_____

Day 274 - Describe the ideal version of yourself when it comes to
your social life (friends).

_____
_____
_____
_____
_____
_____
_____
_____
_____

"No, that is the great fallacy: the wisdom of old men.
They do not grow wise. They grow careful."
Ernest Hemingway

Day 275- Look at yesterday's answer. Write down at least one experience where your social life (friends) was perfect. What can you learn from this experience?

_____
_____
_____
_____
_____
_____
_____
_____
_____
_____

Day 276- What would you like to learn about other people?

_____
_____
_____
_____
_____
_____
_____
_____
_____
_____
_____

*"Sometimes it's not enough to know what things mean,
sometimes you have to know what things don't mean."*
Bob Dylan

Day 277 - What would you regret not tasting if you were going to die today?

_____
_____
_____
_____
_____
_____
_____
_____
_____

Day 278 - How can you best deal with fear for a relapse?

_____
_____
_____
_____
_____
_____
_____
_____
_____
_____
_____

"If opportunity doesn't knock, build a door"
Milton Berle

Day 279- How can you be your own best friend after a relapse?

_____
_____
_____
_____
_____
_____
_____
_____

Day 280 - What can you do to strengthen your recovery this month?

_____
_____
_____
_____
_____
_____
_____
_____
_____
_____
_____
_____

"Take it moment by moment, and you will find that we are all, as I've said before, bugs in amber."
Kurt Vonnegut

Day 281 - How are you most frequently criticize yourself?

_____

_____

_____

_____

_____

_____

_____

_____

Day 282- Look at yesterday's answer and write down the positive counterparts for a maximum of five negative statements. Do it in a way that works for you. For example, 'I never finish anything,' "I am brave enough to try new things."

_____

_____

_____

_____

_____

_____

_____

_____

_____

_____

"Knowledge comes, but wisdom lingers."
Alfred Lord Tennyson

Day 283- Write a response to your critical self for this thought:
"Don't make such a fool out of yourself."

_____

_____

_____

_____

_____

_____

_____

_____

_____

Day 284 - What is your opinion about hard work?

_____

_____

_____

_____

_____

_____

_____

_____

_____

_____

_____

*"I am not a person of opinions
because I feel the counter arguments too strongly."*
Mary Shelley

Day 285 - What are you ashamed of about your family?

Day 286 - How did your viewpoints about recovery change in
the past few years?

"You will not be punished for your anger;
you will be punished by your anger.
Siddhārtha Gautama

Day 287 - What is one problem you had this week? How did you solve it?

_____

_____

_____

_____

_____

_____

_____

_____

_____

Day 288 - What is one mini-goal you can set today?

_____

_____

_____

_____

_____

_____

_____

_____

_____

_____

"I used to think the worst thing in life is to end up all alone. It's not. The worst thing in life is to end up with people who make you feel all alone."
Robin Williams

Day 289 - What did you learn about yourself during your teenage years?

_____

_____

_____

_____

_____

_____

_____

_____

_____

_____

Day 290 - Describe the ideal version of yourself when it comes to your career.

_____

_____

_____

_____

_____

_____

_____

_____

_____

_____

"It is strange how often a heart must be broken
Before the years can make it wise."
Sara Teasdale

Day 291 - Look at yesterday's answer. Write down at least one experience where your career was perfect. What can you learn from this experience?

_____

_____

_____

_____

_____

_____

_____

_____

Day 292 - How can you laugh about addiction?

_____

_____

_____

_____

_____

_____

_____

_____

_____

_____

"Where wisdom reigns, there is no conflict between thinking and feeling."
Carl Gustav Jung

Day 293 - How did your viewpoints about love and relationships change in the past few years?

_____
_____
_____
_____
_____
_____
_____
_____
_____
_____

Day 294 - What did you learn about yourself this week?

_____
_____
_____
_____
_____
_____
_____
_____
_____
_____
_____

"Prediction is very difficult, especially about the future."
Niels Bohr

Day 295 - Do you feel recovery is hard work? Why or why not?

_____
_____
_____
_____
_____
_____
_____
_____
_____
_____

Day 296 - Three lessons you've learned from addiction.

_____
_____
_____
_____
_____
_____
_____
_____
_____
_____
_____
_____

"You cannot teach a man anything;
you can only help him find it within himself."
Galileo

Day 297 - What would you like to learn about friendship?

_____
_____
_____
_____
_____
_____
_____
_____
_____
_____

Day 298 - What is one big problem you had this year? How did
you solve it?

_____
_____
_____
_____
_____
_____
_____
_____
_____
_____
_____

"In order to rise from its own ashes, a Phoenix first must burn."
Octavia Butler

Day 299 - What are you ashamed of about your friends?

_____

_____

_____

_____

_____

_____

_____

_____

_____

_____

Day 300 - What makes life evil sometimes?

_____

_____

_____

_____

_____

_____

_____

_____

_____

_____

_____

"Faith goes up the stairs that love has built and looks out the windows which hope has opened."
Charles H. Spurgeon

Day 301 - What made you feel grateful this week?

_____
_____
_____
_____
_____
_____
_____
_____
_____
_____

Day 302 - Describe a perfect pattern for recovery.

_____
_____
_____
_____
_____
_____
_____
_____
_____
_____
_____

"May your choices reflect your hopes, not your fears."
Nelson Mandela

Day 303 - How has addiction changed your life?

_____

_____

_____

_____

_____

_____

_____

_____

_____

_____

Day 304 - Write a response to your younger self for this thought: "I have no idea what I should do with my life."

_____

_____

_____

_____

_____

_____

_____

_____

_____

_____

"While there's life, there's hope."
Marcus Tullius Cicero

Day 305 - What are the 20 percent of people or actions that are producing 80 percent of your negative emotional states?

_____

_____

_____

_____

_____

_____

_____

_____

_____

Day 306 - What is something you would like to create?

_____

_____

_____

_____

_____

_____

_____

_____

_____

_____

_____

"My hope still is to leave the world a bit better than when I got here."
Jim Henson

Day 307 - Write a response to your younger self for this thought:
"I just feel I am not good enough."

_____

_____

_____

_____

_____

_____

_____

_____

_____

_____

Day 308 - What is one coping skill you learned this week?

_____

_____

_____

_____

_____

_____

_____

_____

_____

_____

_____

_____

*"That was all a man needed: hope.
It was lack of hope that discouraged a man."*
Charles Bukowski

Day 309 - How did your friends shape you negatively? Write down at least three things.

_____
_____
_____
_____
_____
_____
_____
_____
_____

Day - What would be fun to do during recovery?

_____
_____
_____
_____
_____
_____
_____
_____
_____
_____
_____

"The past is made out of facts... I guess the future is just hope."
Isaac Marion

Day 311 - What questions can you ask yourself when you feel sadness?

_____
_____
_____
_____
_____
_____
_____
_____
_____
_____

Day 312 - How can you tell someone is addicted?

_____
_____
_____
_____
_____
_____
_____
_____
_____
_____

"Conventionality is not morality."
Charlotte Bronte

Day 313 - How can you tell someone is in recovery?

_____
_____
_____
_____
_____
_____
_____
_____
_____
_____

Day 314 - How would you like to improve your wardrobe?

_____
_____
_____
_____
_____
_____
_____
_____
_____
_____
_____
_____

"I found the poems in the fields,
And only wrote them down."
John Clare

Day 315 - What's one problem behavior that you challenged this week, and how did you go about testing it?

_____
_____
_____
_____
_____
_____
_____
_____
_____

Day 316 - What is one goal you can set this week?

_____
_____
_____
_____
_____
_____
_____
_____
_____
_____

"A tamed woman will never leave her mark in the world."
Robert M Drake

Day 317 - What is one of the biggest problems you had in your life? How did you solve it?

_____
_____
_____
_____
_____
_____
_____
_____
_____
_____

Day 318 - Describe what you want to say to your friends.

_____
_____
_____
_____
_____
_____
_____
_____
_____
_____

"Rhythm must have meaning."
Ezra Pound

Day 319 - Seven words to describe your strongest self.

_____
_____
_____
_____
_____
_____
_____
_____
_____
_____

Day 320 - What would you regret not doing if you were going to die today?

_____
_____
_____
_____
_____
_____
_____
_____
_____
_____
_____
_____
_____

"Hope is a force of nature. Don't let anyone tell you different."
Jim Butcher

Day 321 - What did you learn this week?

_____

_____

_____

_____

_____

_____

_____

_____

_____

_____

Day 322 - What is the one thing you want to do this week that
would make you feel proud?

_____

_____

_____

_____

_____

_____

_____

_____

_____

_____

"Hope is the last thing a person does before they are defeated."
Henry Rollins

Day 323 - Describe the ideal version of yourself when it comes to health.

_____
_____
_____
_____
_____
_____
_____
_____

Day 324 - Look at yesterday's answer. Write down at least one experience where your actions resembled the best version of yourself when it came to health. What can you learn from this experience?

_____
_____
_____
_____
_____
_____
_____
_____
_____
_____
_____

"I am no bird, no net ensnares me."
Charlotte Brontë

Day 325 - Write a response to your critical self for this thought: "Try harder."

_____
_____
_____
_____
_____
_____
_____
_____
_____
_____

Day 326 - What has been the influence of boredom to your addiction?

_____
_____
_____
_____
_____
_____
_____
_____
_____
_____

*"It is foolish and wrong to mourn the men who died.
Rather, we should thank God that such men lived."*
George S. Patton Jr.

Day 327 - What can you do to better deal with boredom?

_____
_____
_____
_____
_____
_____
_____
_____
_____
_____

Day 328 - How did your viewpoints about money change in the
past few years?

_____
_____
_____
_____
_____
_____
_____
_____
_____
_____
_____

"The only thing that makes life possible is permanent, intolerable uncertainty: not knowing what comes next."
Ursula K. Le Guin

Day 329- What made you feel proud this week?

_____
_____
_____
_____
_____
_____
_____
_____
_____
_____

Day 330 - What did you learn about yourself this month?

_____
_____
_____
_____
_____
_____
_____
_____
_____
_____
_____
_____

"What do we live for, if it is not to make life less difficult for each other?"
George Eliot

Day 331 - What is the most challenging part about recovery for
you? How could you make this easier for yourself?

_____

_____

_____

_____

_____

_____

_____

_____

_____

Day 332 - Write a response to your addiction for this thought:
"We can continue, but just try to control it more."

_____

_____

_____

_____

_____

_____

_____

_____

_____

_____

"Watch and pray, dear, never get tired of trying,
and never think it is impossible to conquer your fault."
Louisa May Alcott

Day 333 - What would you like to learn about health?

_____

_____

_____

_____

_____

_____

_____

_____

_____

_____

Day 334 - What three things would your 80-year-old self tell you to do?

_____

_____

_____

_____

_____

_____

_____

_____

_____

_____

"What we cannot bear removes us from life;
what remains can be borne."
Marcus Aurelius

Day 335 - List up to 5 affirmations to live your life by.

_____
_____
_____
_____
_____
_____
_____
_____
_____
_____

Day 336 - Describe what you want to say to your family.

_____
_____
_____
_____
_____
_____
_____
_____
_____
_____
_____
_____

"Forever is composed of nows."
Emily Dickinson

Day 337 - Three lessons you've learned from recovery so far.

_____
_____
_____
_____
_____
_____
_____
_____
_____
_____
_____

Day 338 - Write a response to your younger self for this thought: "But I don't have the money for it..."

_____
_____
_____
_____
_____
_____
_____
_____
_____
_____
_____
_____

"You just go on your nerve."
Frank O'Hara

Day 339 - Describe the ideal version of yourself when it comes to your creativity.

_____

_____

_____

_____

_____

_____

_____

_____

Day 340 - Look at yesterday's answer. Write down at least one experience where you felt your creativity was making you happy. What can you learn from this experience?

_____

_____

_____

_____

_____

_____

_____

_____

_____

_____

"I dwell in possibility..."
Emily Dickinson

Day 341 - What has been the influence of seeking approval to your addiction?

_____
_____
_____
_____
_____
_____
_____
_____
_____
_____

Day 342 - What did you want to be when you grew up? Why?

_____
_____
_____
_____
_____
_____
_____
_____
_____
_____

"The best ideas are common property"
Seneca

Day 343 - What would you like to learn about life?

_____
_____
_____
_____
_____
_____
_____
_____
_____
_____

Day 344 - Write a reply to your younger self for this thought:
"Everyone else seems to do good, but I'm such a basket case."

_____
_____
_____
_____
_____
_____
_____
_____
_____
_____
_____

"This above all: to thine own self be true."
William Shakespeare

Day 345 - What would you do if money wasn't an issue?

_____
_____
_____
_____
_____
_____
_____
_____
_____

Day 346 - How would you like to improve your appearance?

_____
_____
_____
_____
_____
_____
_____
_____
_____
_____

"...for love casts out fear, and gratitude can conquer pride."
Louisa May Alcott

Day 347 - Describe one memory you're incredibly grateful for.

_____

_____

_____

_____

_____

_____

_____

_____

_____

_____

Day 348 - What questions can you ask yourself when you feel
worried?

_____

_____

_____

_____

_____

_____

_____

_____

_____

_____

_____

"Whereof one cannot speak, thereof one must be silent."
Ludwig Wittgenstein

Day 349 - What are the 20 percent of people or actions that are producing 80 percent of your happiness?

_____

_____

_____

_____

_____

_____

_____

_____

_____

Day 350 - What makes you feel proud of yourself when you look at last week?

_____

_____

_____

_____

_____

_____

_____

_____

_____

_____

_____

"Even the finest sword plunged into salt water will eventually rust."
Sun Tzu

Day 351 - Write about lost friendships.

_____
_____
_____
_____
_____
_____
_____
_____
_____
_____

Day 352 - What is the one thing you want to do this year that would make you feel proud?

_____
_____
_____
_____
_____
_____
_____
_____
_____
_____

"Doing nothing is better than being busy doing nothing."
Lao Tzu

Day 353 - Write a response to your addiction for this thought:
"It's their fault I am this way."

_____
_____
_____
_____
_____
_____
_____
_____
_____

Day 354 - What do you really, truly want?

_____
_____
_____
_____
_____
_____
_____
_____
_____
_____
_____

"But the cloud never comes in that quarter of the horizon from which we watch for it."
Elizabeth Gaskell

Day 355 - If you had to choose one affirmation to live by this year, what would it be?

_____
_____
_____
_____
_____
_____
_____
_____
_____
_____

Day 356 - What would you like to learn about fame?

_____
_____
_____
_____
_____
_____
_____
_____
_____
_____
_____

"O words are poor receipts for what time hath stole away"
John Clare

Day 357 - What did you learn about yourself this year?

_____

_____

_____

_____

_____

_____

_____

_____

_____

_____

Day 358 - Write about your lost dreams.

_____

_____

_____

_____

_____

_____

_____

_____

_____

_____

_____

"Beauty is not caused. It is."
Emily Dickinson

Day 359 - Write a response to your critical self for this thought:
"You're doing recovery wrong."

_____
_____
_____
_____
_____
_____
_____
_____
_____

Day 360 - If you had to choose one affirmation to live by, what
would it be?

_____
_____
_____
_____
_____
_____
_____
_____
_____
_____
_____

*"I never found beauty in longing for the impossible
and never found the possible to be beyond my reach."*
Ayn Rand

Day 361- What is your life calling?

_____

_____

_____

_____

_____

_____

_____

_____

_____

_____

Day 362 - Who is your authentic self?

_____

_____

_____

_____

_____

_____

_____

_____

_____

_____

_____

*"A man devoid of hope and conscious of being
so has ceased to belong to the future."*
Albert Camus

Day 363 - Who are you becoming?

_____
_____
_____
_____
_____
_____
_____
_____
_____
_____

Day 364 - Write down a thank you letter to yourself, for all the
effort you've put in this year.

_____
_____
_____
_____
_____
_____
_____
_____
_____
_____

"Whenever you get there, there is no there there."
Gertrude Stein

Day 365 - Write down a letter to yourself, opened to be one year from now.

_____

_____

_____

_____

_____

_____

_____

_____

_____

_____

_____

_____

_____

_____

_____

_____

_____

_____

_____

_____

_____

_____

_____

_____

_____

_____

**Thanks for making it to the end.
We wish you all the best.**

2J Exercises

On the following page you find a preview of C.W. V. Straaten's, *The Addiction Recovery Workbook: A 7-Step Master Plan To Take Back Control Of Your Life*

If you want to purchase this workbook, you can find it on Amazon.

The Claws of Addiction

"That you may live every day of your life."

Jonathan Swift

On the surface there was nothing wrong with me. I was renting my own apartment, had a decent job, and a kind face for almost everyone. Each day I went to work, where I behaved like a decent employee. Every weekend I went out with friends and, on more than one occasion, had a few too many drinks. But everyone does, right? I was nice to my family, nice to my neighbours, nice to unknown people in the street. But when I returned to my apartment and locked the door and closed the curtains, I was confronted with my secrets. The debts that kept piling up, loneliness, boredom, and the one solution that numbed all of my problems.

During the Christmas holidays, I had a week off. It was supposed to be a fun time. Days where you don't have to do anything. Socializing with friends, seeing your grandparents for a change, cleaning your room and reading that one book that you've looked forward to for months. All the while the atmosphere in the streets is one of kindness and warmth. Christmas is coming and everyone seems a bit more friendly. Peaceful, but I couldn't see it since the curtains of my apartment were closed.

I was constantly checking my bank account, waiting for the extra salary I was getting in December. It was the 24th of December and I was laying in my bed in my messy apartment with three empty beer cans on my desk, with a pair of trousers and my new, expensive shirt on the ground. I was looking at my phone. 3:11 PM. The money would be there at any moment. And I needed it.

Oh, I desperately needed it. No more than one hour ago did I lose over 300 Euros betting on Dutch soccer. I didn't have a single dime left, not even to buy some Christmas presents. When my salary came in, all of these problems would be solved and I could finally sing along to Paul McCartney's Wonderful Christmastime.

One hour later. Most stores were almost closed. I had to hurry, but I was watching a live soccer match. One more goal and I would win almost 500 Euros. I was still in my bed. The curtains were still closed. It could have been the first of February, or the 13th of October. Does time matter in the hour of desperation? In the distance I heard an ambulance and the notes of a well known Christmas melody. I needed one goal. It would solve my financial situation. It would solve my depression. It would solve everything.

Three minutes were left to play. I thought about my family, I thought about the calmness, the serene feelings that were coming along with these days. And boy, did I want to be a part of it. Time was ticking indifferently. It's unbelievable to believe that you could lose an entire paycheck within one hour. You could lose everything you hold dear, for that matter, within one hour. Addiction has the enormous power to destroy conscientiousness and sensibility. It is a storm that could destroy what one has built up for months within mere minutes.

A shout, a curse. A slap against the wall. It's time. No goal. No money. No solution anymore. I watch my laptop screen in agony. The screen turns black: the live stream is over. I check my account balance, just to be certain. There it is, an indifferent, cold zero.

Your Lowest Point In Life

We addicts, or people with seriously detrimental bad habits, all know of situations like this. Maybe not as dramatic, or maybe way more dramatic. We know the stories of the husband that steals his children's college money to feed his gambling habits, or a mother that continues to drug herself while raising her children, or the boss who sexually intimidates his employees. Tough stories that speak to the imagination. It's what we link addiction to. Alcohol, drugs, gambling, sex.

But what about the millions of people who suffer from bad habits in the confidence and security of their own homes?

Housewives playing Facebook games for hours a day, the young professional who binge watches Netflix every night, the young student who spends entire days checking social media. And so on. These habits might seem a bit more trivial, but they all have the same effect: you don't see the real problem any more.

Every bad habit and every addiction serves a purpose. It grants you instantaneous pleasure. You can attain it without much effort. It won't take any effort to grab a fourth beer on Tuesday night, eat your third piece of apple pie in the middle of the night, or play that video game. (Only in the last stages of a destroying addiction does it become difficult to continue the habit, due to either a lack of money, the possibility that others might find out, or because you've made it difficult for yourself to continue. For example, not being in control of your own money anymore).

"People are not meant to be on this earth just to fight an addiction."

Back to my gambling story. Unfortunately that wasn't the last time I gambled, but it was one of my last episodes. I've lost tens of thousands of Euros over my seven years of gambling. I lost an insane number of hours aimlessly watching live sporting streams in the middle of night, tired and irritated while losing over and over again. There were points where continuing to smile seemed to be an option no more. Times where I couldn't see the near future.. But somehow, whenever I woke up the next day I always had a feeling that this couldn't be what life was all about. That this wasn't the purpose. That there should be more. Much, much more. No, people are not meant to be on this earth just to fight an addiction.

It was only when I truly understood why I gambled, and when I could replace my addictive thoughts and behaviour with positive and constructive ones that disrupted the addictive pattern that real and lasting changes occurred. Now, I haven't gambled in over four years. My life has gone from debt, loneliness, and a messy apartment with closed curtains, to a rich and fulfilled life. I've used the strategy that I used to break my addiction to break other bad habits (which means either stopping it altogether or simply refraining from overindulging), such as drinking too much on a Saturday night and watching over two hours a day of television.

Now I want to share the strategy that worked successfully for me, with the rest of the world.

I've written this workbook, first and foremost, for you, the struggling addict. I wrote it because I know from experience that it can destroy your life. I wrote it because I can't stand to see so many wonderful souls being torn down by the devilish claws of addiction. I wrote it, because I know there is a way out. Even for the worst struggling addict.

Just quitting your addiction is one thing. It is what you get back when you quit or no longer overindulge in something that you feel true joy. Besides the incredible change in my financial situation, health, productivity, and social life, the change I am most excited about is the change in my consciousness. Finally, I feel strong, secure and self-confident enough to experience life fully. I'm no longer in my head all the time, which allows me to finally connect with the people I love so much, as well as new people. I can enjoy the fruits of life with integrity, as I can respond to any personal problems in a strong and constructive manner. This feeling of control, of enjoying life and most importantly, of truly connecting with other people, is worth every struggle that the gambling addiction brought to my life.

This workbook is not only intended to help you with quitting your addiction. It is also intended to help you to start over. To create and *live* the life you deserve. Because, after all, don't you at least deserve to experience a bit more joy than the chains of addiction?

How to Read This Workbook

With this step-by-step workbook, I want to inspire and help you to take back control over your own life by not letting addiction be the guiding force of your life anymore. This book shares the same 7 simple steps I went through to quit my destructive habit: gambling addiction. I made it a structured and practical workbook that is intended to help you instantly or at the very least inspire you to take the steps necessary for you. The book guides you into the better understanding of your addiction. The reason *why* addiction is present in *your* life. Most importantly, this workbook will give you tools to solve problems your addiction has caused and to be proactive in creating a meaningful, joyful life. A life where you will be strong and secure enough to deal with the inevitable problems of life. And where you will deal with these problems consciously, without hiding in the horrific claws of addiction.

The time indicated under the steps is, of course, a mere indication. It could help to follow this timetable, in order to make your addiction process more attainable. If for whatever reason you won't go cold turkey or your goal is only to stop overindulging in your addictive behaviour, I absolutely welcome you aboard. I want to inspire you to take back control of your life. For almost all addicts that eventually means quitting altogether. But it's up to you. Take your time if you need it.

As we all know, recovery doesn't simply require the fulfillment of some steps.

Especially when accounting for the processes of revealing what kind of feelings you are trying to hide by turning to your addiction, recovery is a procedure that could take months. And for some much, much longer. But even in a shorter period of time, you can take giant steps to proactively deal with the consequences of your addiction, building up inner strength to combat your addictive cravings. And most importantly you can find meaning in your life by working on your talents, connecting with others and enjoying life to the fullest.

I would recommend to immediately start with the guided 90-Day Journal on page 79. These daily writing prompts will surely help to improve the recovery process, better understand your addiction, and strengthen the relationship with yourself. I would recommend to reflect on one question each day and read and use the workbook simultaneously.

Note to the Reader

As stated in the disclaimer, this book is not intended to act as a substitute for medical advice or treatment. Any person with a condition requiring medical attention should consult a qualified medical practitioner or suitable therapist. Addiction can sometimes become physical, especially when you have a severe alcohol or drug addiction. Also when suffering from severe mental problems, it is wise to contact a suitable therapist. Listen to yourself and to your body, and never be too proud to ask for help.

A book is merely a book. Words are merely words. In and of themselves, they bear no magic. But you, within yourself, have the power to transform words. Into hope. Into better thoughts. Into better actions. And eventually, into change.

Don't be discouraged when you don't see overnight results. Because that's not the purpose of this book. And, I guess, that's not the purpose of any recovery method. Addiction is a giant that can only be taken down by small steps. If the only thing you get out of this book is a clearer and stronger intent on why you want to quit your addiction and how you're going to do it, that's perfectly fine.

For some this book, these words will bring more. Discover what it brings to you. And remember, don't be too hard for yourself. Please don't. A little love to yourself can go a long way. It is the announcement of a new dawn. And I sincerely hope that this book will help you to find that new dawn. To eventually stop addiction. Put an end to it. Find recovery. And then, find a new life. Your life.

Step 1 - Quitting The Pattern

Day 1

The first step in your journey to a new life without addiction is a simple one. Just don't do it anymore. Don't smoke your cigarette anymore, stop going to the casino, stop overeating. Simple, right?

Simple, yes. Easy, no. Not at all.

Quitting your addiction might as well be one of the hardest things in the world. It means conquering an ingrained habit. It means changing something that you've been doing day in and day out, for a long period of time. It has become second nature. And whatever we say about addiction, it is something that has helped you enormously over the last few years. It has protected you when you needed it most. The addiction numbed your deep feelings of pain. But since you've purchased this workbook, you and I both know that those days are numbered. No longer is the addiction the solution. The addiction is an even worse place, despite its distraction from your deepest pains. Today will be the first step on your journey to change. Wake up from this nightmare. Meet your new dan.

In step 1 of this workbook we will go over these 4 points that will help quit your addictive pattern. These can very well be the start of your new, addiction-free life.

Quitting our addiction? Do it smart.
- **Share your story.**

- **Stop.**
- **Seek help.**
- **Cut off resources.**

Quitting your addiction? Do it smart.

This is really important. As stated in the disclaimer and in the note to the reader, this book is not intended to act as a substitute for medical advice or treatment. Take this statement to heart. Going cold turkey isn't always safe when your addiction has become physical, such as in cases of alcohol or drugs. Keep this in mind. I was a heavy gambler, a true addict. I've tried to lessen my gambling behaviour before, but at a certain moment that simply wasn't helpful anymore. The only solution for me was to quit altogether. Find your way. Be honest with yourself. Quitting your addiction? Do it smart. And it's you who, deep inside, always knows best.

Share, stop and seek help.

One of the biggest breakthroughs I had during my recovery process was sharing my story. It was just after I had made an attempt to quit gambling altogether. This unfortunately wasn't my last attempt, but the sharing of my story was crucial in eventually conquering my addiction for good. It was on a Wednesday night, just the day before I went through a long and devastating gambling period. I lost almost 2000 Euros, which was a lot of money for me at that time. When I woke up the following day, I decided - no more! That night I called one of my dear friends. After some preliminary chit chat, I was finally courageous enough to share the real reason for my phone call.

"I have a problem, and it's been going on for quite some time now. It's a gambling problem."

I was at my parents' house at the time. Nobody was home. I remember walking through the house while telling the story. My friend listened, as the very best of friends tend to do, and he offered help. It was after one more relapse that I decided to take his help. Yet sharing my addiction story was one of the best feelings I had during those dark years of gambling. It lifted the weight off my back and eventually reassured me that I didn't have to be on this journey all by myself.

That's why my advice is to share your story.

It will take courage, but it will be a huge step to freedom - to breaking down your addiction. If there is someone in your life that you can share it with, someone that won't judge you, then that just might be the person to which you can tell your story. But practice the conversation in your head. This will make it easier when you have to do it in real life. Additionally, discussing the issue over a phone call might be easier than doing it face to face. If you don't have a friend, family member or someone else to call, share it somewhere else. There are online forums or Facebook groups for people with your addiction, where you can share your story either anonymously or not. Alternatively, you could share it with a professional, anonymously with a professional helpline (telephone or chat), or a support group.

This first step, like any other first step, could easily be the most difficult one. Sharing your dark, long-kept secret may be one of the most challenging hurdles you'll ever overcome. And it's worth the struggle. By sharing it, the heavy pressure of your addiction will feel lighter, and all of a sudden you're not alone in your fight anymore.

Stop.

If you want to quit your addiction, there is no other way than to first say: 'It's over now, I'll quit.' Even if your purpose is only to lessen your addictive behaviour (for example by only gambling once per week with a specific budget, smoking three cigarettes a day, or drinking only two glasses of alcohol and only on the weekend), it's a great first step to stop altogether with your addictive behaviour for a period of time. It's crucial to be one hundred percent behind your decision to quit. If you're a spiritual person, it will help to ask your God for help in this process. If you're not spiritual, ask your Higher Self to guide and guard you in the quitting process.

The conscious decision of quitting your addiction, and actually stopping your addictive behaviour, are steps that are attainable for all addicts (except when it's a physical addiction and you need medical assistance). I absolutely believe that every addict, whether suffering from an addiction to pornograpy or overeating, social media or gaming, can stop his or her addiction for at least 24 hours. If you do it right, I am quite certain that you'll be able to add another 24 hours.

And another.

> *"When you make the conscious decision*
> *to quit your addiction,*
> *don't make it solely about the quitting itself;*
> *try to see what you could gain."*

Don't make it harder for yourself than it needs to be. Only the act of reaching that first milestone of 24 hours should give you a reason to celebrate. So celebrate if you've made it to the first 24 hours, celebrate again when you make it to 48 hours, and so on. Do this for at least one week. Find a healthy pleasure that isn't your addiction, like watching a movie with friends, taking a walk in nature, or buying yourself a little present. We'll discuss these options further in step 2.

I know the horrors of addiction. That's why the quitting process should be something wonderful. Of course there are lots of responsibilities to attend to after you've quit, like financial consequences, health problems, needing another diet, and deteriorated relationships. And of course, we'll deal with these problems in step 3. But there's more. When you make a conscious decision to quit your addiction, don't make it solely about the quitting itself; try to see what you could gain. A life of freedom, however you define that for yourself. Wearing that beautiful dress with confidence, being able to buy you friends dinner, being in a great condition, having a wonderful night out without being mean, because you're drunk or on drugs, and so on. That joyous and compelling dream or, when you haven't really defined your ideal life yet, at least the absence of addictive horrors will move you forward in the first days of quitting your addiction.

Seek help.

> *"Ask for help. Not because you are weak.*
> *But because you want to remain strong."*

Les Brown

When you've made the decision to quit, don't be alone. You could share your decision with the friend, family, professional worker or group you've contacted to talk about your addiction. Asking for help doesn't make you weak; it is the only smart way to know your weaknesses and give yourself the extra power of another person or support group to fight something as big as an addiction.

Define for yourself how you want to be helped. For example, the option of calling someone when you're having a really hard time with your addictive thoughts, having an accountability buddy, or simply ask the other person/support group what they suggest. For most addicts, it is one bridge too far to really seek professional help, and yes, there are other ways to do it. But it's going to be hard to do it all on your own. So at least share your story and find the courage to ask for help in whatever way suits you best. Like we went over in *Share your story*, you could also do it anonymously, online, or with a professional helpline.

Cut off resources.

What's critical in the quitting process is cutting off from resources that fuel your addiction. These could mean access to your money, to certain websites, to unhealthy food, alcohol, casinos, etc. By cutting yourself off from these resources, you will make it so much easier on yourself to actually follow through on your recovery. You could do this together with the person or group you've gone to for help.

When I made my final attempt to quit my gambling addiction, more than four years ago, I asked my good friend to take control of my bank account. He took over my banking passes and access to online banking. If you make it difficult for yourself to indulge in your addictive behaviour again, you have a better chance of succeeding.

If you want to you can find a **healthy** substitute for these resources. I still had some money, but it was cash money that my friend gave me. Or instead of bottles of wine, have bottles of a healthy soda you absolutely like, and so on. Don't change a bad habit for another bad habit. But use your imagination and pick something from the thousands of positive, healthy options this universe has to offer.

A Last word of Encouragement + Empowering Exercise

It's very easy to start blaming yourself during this period. It can be devastating thinking about all the problems you've caused with your addiction... Stop for a moment and consider your achievement of this day.

The day you quit. The day you stood up to your addiction. The day you said no the destructive and the decline and yes to a richer, more authentic life. To a new beginning.

You need to be your own best friend in this period (and for the rest of your life). Pat yourself on the back for taking this enormous step to committing to quitting your addiction forever. It's probably the most courageous thing you've done in your life so far.

Statements Exercise

A good way to emphasize this is by putting empowering statements/affirmations on sticky notes around your home or on your smartphone. There are countless free affirmation apps for your smartphone that can help you with this! A good exercise for now is to come up with at least 5 to 10 empowering statements/affirmations that will guide you through the initial stages of your recovery.

So why not do it right now. Sit down and write statements that speak to *you*.

Hereby a couple of examples:

There is so much more to life than the pain and suffering from addiction.

Addiction is a waste of my time.

Life in recovery is absolutely authentic for me.

Addiction is a lie, my spirit is the truth of recovery.

Only a fool waits for addiction to make him/her happy

Addiction is killing my energy for life, recovery is my new energy.

The Universe/God is guiding me from the darkness of addiction into the light of recovery.

Recovery from the lies of addiction is my new way of life.

I am so much more than the destruction of addiction.

There are thousands of positive, creative options to spend your time on in life.

There are a lot of rules for affirmations, but just write down what **you feel is right**. Sometimes *negative* affirmations, such as 'Affirmation is killing my time', can be extremely helpful in the beginning stages of fighting an addiction. Especially when you mix it with positive statements.

The next level is to record your statements on your smartphone and listen to your statements/affirmations over and over again. When you go to work, when you cook, before you go to sleep, when you sleep, and so on. Change your thoughts, and you diminish the power of addiction significantly. To make it even better, you can put on some music under your statements to emphasize these statements. Search for 'audio mix' in the play store or apple store to easily mix your statements with motivational music (instrumental music, such as movie soundtracks is highly recommended).

I added this exercise because, after the initial setup, it can be easily done without much effort. Just simply put in your earphones and go for a walk. Give your mind a different tape to listen to, than the destructive thought patterns of addiction. Listening to the statements can also bring up emotions, especially when you mix it with inspirational music (such as movie soundtracks). This can open up the possibility to release and confront the emotions around addiction. And find new passion, more intention for change.

Of course this *statement exercise* alone won't override your addictive thoughts. It's only a tool to help you during recovery. To emphasize where you don't want to go and where you *do* want to go. But you need more than affirmations to change. So we're going to find the patterns. To educate ourselves. To take responsibility. To find a new vision. And eventually we then can discover lasting change. So try out this exercise a couple of times for yourself, see how it works for you.

Because when it comes to recovery in general, there are no guru's. There are just teachers that can bring you to the truth within.

Who can show you ways or methods to release thoughts, powers, that are holding back who you really are. The utmost reason why I would like you to try out this exercise is my belief that changing your thoughts almost always changes your reality. And, as all the exercises in this book have benefited me, this one especially has helped me enormously in my own recovery.

Summary - Step 1

- *Quitting your addiction? Do it smart.* Read the disclaimer of this book and the note to the reader.
- *Share your story.* Don't pull the full weight of your addiction all on your own. Find someone to share your story with.
- *Stop.* However you want to deal with your addiction, quitting it altogether first is the best way to conquer it. Stop and celebrate every day, for one week at least, that you've made this first step. Make it not only about quitting your addiction, but also about what you will gain when you quit.
- *Seek help.* In whatever way suits you best. It's really hard to quit totally on your own. *"Ask for help. Not because you are weak. But because you want to remain strong."*
- *Cutting off resources.* If you make it difficult for yourself to indulge in your addictive behaviour again, you have a better chance of succeeding.
- *Statements/Affirmation exercise.* For changing your thoughts, almost always changes your reality.

The 365
Addiction Recovery Journal

Follow us on Instagram
For promotions, giveaways and newest arrivals

Instagram:
2lexercises_journals

Made in United States
Orlando, FL
11 November 2024

53746857R00136